WORLD OF SPORTS

SNOWBOARDING

Published by Smart Apple Media

1980 Lookout Drive, North Mankato, Minnesota 56003

Photographs by AllSport (Nathan Bilow), Brunswick
Corporation, Icon Sports Media (Robert Beck, Jim Gund),
Gunter Marx Photography, Dan Sherwood, Sports-
Chrome (Bongarts Photography, Sport the Library),
Sports Gallery (Al Messerschmidt), Unicorn (Dave Lyons,
Jim Shippee)

Design and production by EvansDay Design

LIBRARY OF CONGRESS CATALOGING-IN-PUBLICATION DATA

McAuliffe, Bill.
Snowboarding / by Bill McAuliffe.
p. cm. — (World of sports)
Includes index.
Summary: Describes the history, equipment, and
techniques of snowboarding.
ISBN 1-58340-163-6
1. Snowboarding—Juvenile literature. [1. Snowboarding.]
I. Title. II. World of sports (North Mankato, Minn.).

GV857 .S57 M363 2002
796.93'9–dc21   2001049966

First Edition
9 8 7 6 5 4 3 2 1

SNOW BOARDING

BILL McAULIFFE

With a couple of quick tugs, I'm buckled into my bindings and raring to go. I hop once to turn the board downhill and take off. In seconds I'm flowing down the fall line. Surfing the slopes. The board floats from one turn to the next, my body rising and sinking in rhythm with the turns. Total freedom. I spot a small jump to one side of the trail, hit a backside air, and stick the landing before melting back into the ride. Moments later, I slow to a relaxing glide as the mountain rolls out into the valley.

Jeff Bennett, SNOWBOARDER AND AUTHOR

The Long, White Ride

I━━━━I

The ride up the chair lift is suspenseful. You're eager to test everything you've learned from your friends and instructors. Can you remember it all? As the lift rises high above the hill, snowboarders streak down the steep slope below you. They draw long, grace- *Snowboarding exploded in* fully curving lines behind them like brush *popularity in the 1990s.* strokes on a canvas. Some lean so far into their *From 1990 to 2000, the* turns they nearly skim the snow with a shoul- *number of snowboarders* der. Others loop their way down, gliding first *in the United States nearly* *tripled, to an estimated 4.3* *million, according to the* *National Sporting Goods* *Association.*

forward, then backward like skaters. Is it the height of the chair lift or the excitement that makes your stomach turn a little?

At the top of the mountain, you scoot off the chair lift and over to a bench so you can snap your free foot onto your board. The sun lights the snow and dark pools of forest on the surrounding peaks. The cold winter air feels clean as you inhale deeply.

You look downhill at the wide, white slope. The lodge below, where some of your friends are still hanging out, looks tiny. You can hardly hear the music on the loudspeakers. This is the easy slope, but still you wonder what it will take to get to the bottom. You know you'll feel different once you get there.

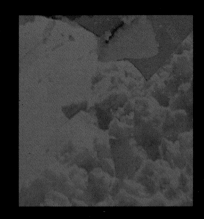

Terry Kidwell has been called the "father of freestyle snowboarding." A former water skier, he started developing tricks on a snowboard in 1980 and won four world championships by the time he retired in the late 1980s.

You start out slowly, riding sideways across the hill, leaning slightly backwards on your heels. When you're near the trees on one side of the run, you shift your weight, pull your back foot a little downhill, and change direction, back across the hill. So far, so good.

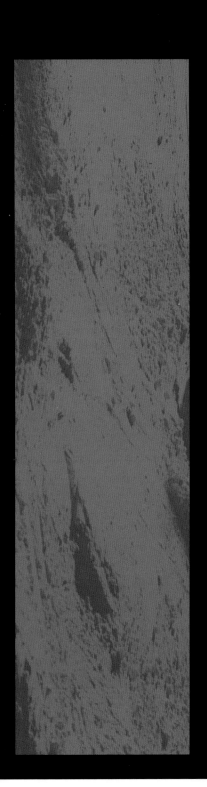

Next, you dare yourself to try a turn. With a slight twist of your body, you rock from your heels to your toes, and the board swings around with you. But it doesn't swing quite far enough. Suddenly, you're heading more downhill than across it. You pick up speed. You bend your knees, spread your hands for balance, and notice you're approaching those trees pretty fast.

A bump rocks you forward. Your board angles up, the edge digs in, and suddenly you're turning sharply uphill. The movement is confusing and throws you off balance. The next thing you know, you have a face full of cold, wet snow.

The friend who rode up with you laughs as she rides by. But who cares? That was exciting! You push yourself up again and brush the snow off, ea-ger to get back that feeling you had—if for just a second—of gliding on air.

New snowboards typically cost between $200 and $500, not including boots and bindings. But bargain hunters can cut the cost by shopping sales and buying quality used equipment.

Carefully, you head back across the hill, leaning into a few turns again where the slope isn't so steep. You fall a couple more times. By the time you reach the bottom, your friend is already impatient to get back on the chair lift. You know just how she feels. "Let's go!" you say. Together, you join the long line of snowboarders at the lift, ready for more **shredding**.

An Explosion in Popularity

■━━━━■

Thousands of years ago, when the Egyptians were building the pyramids, people in the **Arctic** regions were strapping skis on their feet so they could move across the snow and hunt more efficiently. Images of humans using skis and poles were carved onto cave walls in eastern Russia 7,000 to 9,000 years ago. Vikings also skied for fun about 1,000 years ago and wrote poetry about it.

But snowboarding was developed less than 50 years ago in the United States. In the early 1960s, an eighth-grade shop student named Tom Sims

Snowboarders are often required to wear a leash, or strap, that connects the board to their front leg. The leash prevents a board from sliding downhill after a snowboarder falls.

developed a **laminated** wood board with an aluminum bottom and called it a skateboard for snow. Sims later became a major designer and manufacturer of skateboards and snowboards.

Sims was still in high school when Sherman Poppen, a Michigan inventor who worked for a sports equipment company, saw his daughter try to go down a hill while standing up on a sled. Poppen screwed

Arctic *the far northern part of the world*

laminated *pressed into one solid piece*

IT HAS ONLY RECENTLY BLOSSOMED IN POPULARITY, BUT SNOWBOARDING HAS BEEN EVOLVING FOR DECADES.

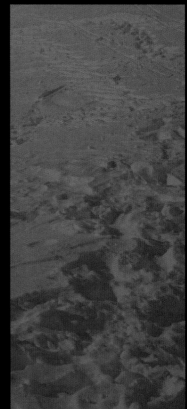

two skis together to make a platform. He drove small nails up through the ski bottoms so his daughter's feet had something to grip. Then he tied a rope to the front so she could stand and steer. His wife called it a Snurfer—a snow surfer.

The Snurfer gained some popularity. In fact, in 1968, downhill Snurfer races were held in Michigan. That same year, a 14-year-old boy in Vermont named Jake Burton Carpenter got a Snurfer for Christmas. Carpenter quickly became a good Snurfer rider and soon began making changes to the board.

A stomp pad is a rough piece of material between bindings. It allows snowboarders to maintain a grip on the board when their back foot is out of its binding, usually while pushing across a flat area.

INTRODUCED IN THE
1960S, THE SNURFER
HELPED PROPEL THE
DEVELOPMENT OF
SNOWBOARDING.

powder *deep, fluffy, freshly fallen snow*

bindings *devices with clips or straps that keep a snowboarder's feet attached to the board*

About the same time, a surfer named Dimitrije Milovich, who was living in Utah, developed a plastic surfboard for snow. He started a company in 1975 to produce boards with spoon-shaped noses and various types of tails. Milovich went out of business by 1984, but in the meantime, Sims, who had become a world-class skateboarder,

To keep from getting too warm or too cold, snowboarders wear layers of clothing and add to them or remove them as necessary. Wearing too little clothing or clothes that are damp can make a snowboarder danger-ously cold.

had developed a long snowboard. With its V-shaped tail, the board worked well in deep **powder**.

In 1977, Carpenter started a snowboard manufacturing company called Burton Snowboards. His boards featured steel edges, adjustable **bindings**, and a smooth plastic coating on the bottom. In 1979, he won the last Snurfer race ever held. He also introduced a Burton snowboard into the competition. Today, Burton Snowboards is one of the world's largest snowboard manufacturers.

Snowboards allowed riders to ski without poles and to go backwards. As was true of skateboards, snowboards also let riders do a wide variety of jumps and tricks. Snowboards caught on quickly, particularly with young people. But skiers didn't like sharing the slopes with snowboarders. They thought snowboarders were reckless, discourteous, and unpredictable. Many ski hills did not allow snowboarders to use their slopes.

As the sport rapidly gained popularity throughout the 1980s, however, rules began to change. Many parents who skied found that their children liked snowboarding better. They started asking ski hill operators to allow their children to snowboard while they skied.

HAND INJURIES ARE NOT UNCOMMON WHILE NOVICE SNOWBOARDERS ARE LEARNING TO MAINTAIN BALANCE.

In 1983, major resorts at Breckenridge, Colorado, and Stratton Mountain, Vermont, began accepting snowboarders. Two years later, only five percent of all of the nation's mountain resorts allowed snowboarding. But in 1987, snowboarding's popularity exploded, and snowboarders were shredding freely at 95 percent of the ski hills in the United States.

For all-purpose snowboarding, snowboarders up to 130 pounds (59 kg) should use a 55-inch (140 cm) board. Add three inches (8 cm) for each additional 15 to 20 pounds (7–9 kg), up to 63 inches (160 cm).

Today, it's not unusual to find ski hills where snowboarders outnumber skiers. Although those ancient Arctic hunters were far more familiar with walking than with surfing and skateboarding, it's a wonder snowboarding didn't come along sooner.

15

Selecting the Right Gear

◾▬◾

As is the case with any sport, equipment that fits right, works right, and is safe can make snowboarding a lot more fun. But there are many, many options. With their vivid colors and explosive patterns, snowboards are built to catch the eye as they dart and swoop across wintry mountain landscapes. Up close, they are a sophisticated combination of art and science.

In 1999, more than half of all snowboarders in the United States were younger than 18 years old. By comparison, more than half of all alpine skiers were older than 25.

Modern snowboards are generally made of laminated layers of fiberglass molded around a wooden core. Different combinations of these materials provide flexibility that helps boarders match their height and weight to the type of snowboarding they want to do. The boards also have metal edges to cut into the snow and a smooth, hard plastic base to reduce **friction**.

Snowboards measure about 40 to 80 inches (100–200 cm) in length. Because snowboarders stand sideways, like surfers, the boards are wide enough to keep the boarders' heels and toes from catching in the snow—a sure way to take a tumble! Shorter snowboards turn quickly

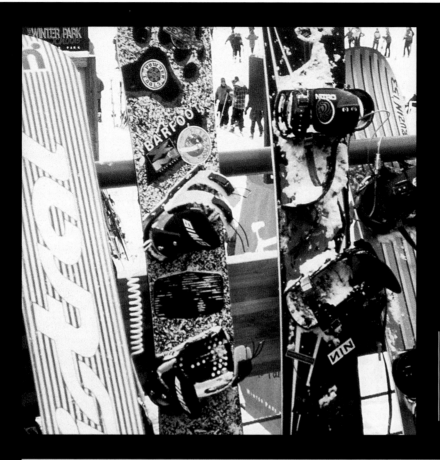

friction *the rubbing or dragging of one surface against another*

freestyle *snowboarding that emphasizes tricks, jumps, and other maneuvers*

carving *making turns on a downhill run that slice into the snow rather than skid across it*

freeriding *all-terrain snowboarding; it combines some jumping with general downhill riding*

BOARDS ARE DESIGNED TO FIT A BOARDER'S SIZE AND STYLE—AND DECORATED ACCORDING TO PERSONAL TASTES.

and are preferred for **freestyle** boarding, which emphasizes jumps and tricks. Longer snowboards are better for **carving** and **freeriding**.

Snowboards have many different shapes. Short freestyle boards often have "twin tips," which means the nose and tail have the same rounded, tipped-up shape to allow for quick changes of direction. This design is ideal for riding backwards, or "fakie," doing quick turns, spins and jumps, and for acrobatic routines in the **halfpipe**. Freestyle boards are also "soft," or flexible, which helps beginning riders.

Freeriding boards are longer, stiffer, and narrower in the middle. This shape is good for carving and all-purpose snowboarding. Alpine boards are the longest and narrowest. They're designed for snowboarders who want to rip down mountainsides at high speeds and offer holding control on even the hardest packed snow or ice. Snowboards specifically designed for women, who are often lighter for their height than men, are now becoming more common.

As the sport spins off into international competitions and receives greater exposure on television and in videos, more and more boards are being marketed as "professional models." These carry endorsements by well-known snowboarding champions and stars.

*Snowboarding, like any sport, has certain "rules of etiquette." For example, snowboarders should plan their run down the hill in advance and stay in control. They also should give the **right of way** to people going downhill ahead of them.*

Part of the reason for snowboarding's popularity may be the boots. Most boots used in snowboarding are soft and warm. Because they're more like regular winter boots than hard ski boots, boarders can walk around in them. In many designs, liners can be inflated to provide the right fit for any foot. At the end of a long day, the liners can be removed and dried. Designers are constantly developing quicker and easier ways to fasten or tighten boots.

Snowboarders who like the thrill of speed and carving down long, sometimes icy slopes generally use hard-shell boots like modern ski boots. These provide a lot of ankle support when riders make high-speed turns.

SNOWBOARDING BOOTS MUST FIT SNUGLY AND—TOGETHER WITH THE BINDINGS—PROVIDE GOOD ANKLE SUPPORT.

halfpipe *a long trough with a rounded bottom and vertical walls that snowboarders ride through from side to side, often flying above the walls and doing tricks in the air*

right of way *the right to proceed unimpeded ahead of others on a path or slope*

19

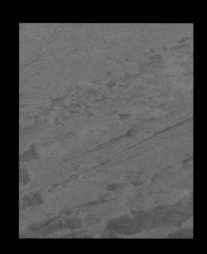

Snowboarders must have one foot free to push themselves across flat ground, as if they were skateboarding, but they fix both feet to the board in bindings when they're ready to head downhill. Most bindings have high backs to support the heel and ankle in soft boots. Straps on top of the foot were common features on bindings for many years, but they required boarders to sit in the snow and often remove their gloves to get strapped in.

Most snowboarders lead with their left foot. This is considered the "regular" stance. Leading with the right foot is called riding "goofy." Some of the world's best riders are goofy.

Today, step-in bindings, much like the bindings on some bicycle pedals, are becoming common. They can be adjusted more precisely, don't squeeze the feet, and can be clipped into while boarders are standing. A new type of binding even allows snow-

ONE OF THE MOST BASIC DIFFERENCES IN BOARDING STYLES IS WHETHER BOARDERS RIDE REGULAR OR GOOFY.

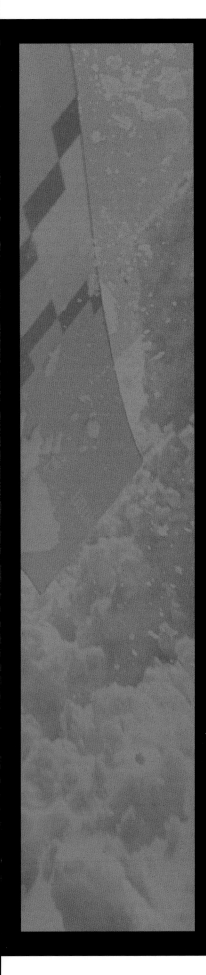

boarders to change the angle of their front foot with the kick of a switch. With most bindings, the front foot remains fixed at an angle to the board. This new device allows snowboarders to ride chair lifts or push across flat areas more comfortably.

Snowboarders who have fallen forward can place the board firmly on their downhill side, then walk themselves upright with their hands. If they've fallen backwards, they can roll over and walk themselves up with their hands.

In addition to equipment, style also is important. Style refers to what boarders can do on their boards and what they wear. Most snowboarders are easy to distinguish from skiers. They wear baggy pants and long, loose jackets, or even layers of shirts and T-shirts. While the clothes might look like street clothes, some are designed specifically for snowboarding. Pants, for example, sometimes are padded in the seat and knees to help cushion falls. Gloves or mittens sometimes have a strap that helps to protect against wrist injuries.

Alpine and competitive snowboarders, who put a premium on speed, usually wear sleeker clothing, much like skiers. Otherwise, snowboarders wear items everyone finds useful on the mountain: goggles, to reduce glare and wind in the eyes, and backpacks, to carry food, tools, and clothing they've either taken off or might put on. Helmets are a good idea for rides on ice or hardpack, but a warm hat is always a necessity, regardless of terrain.

A Steep Learning Curve

Seasoned skiers who have taken up snowboarding say snowboarding is initially harder to learn but easier to improve on after the first few lessons. "You fall a lot at first," said one 25-year-old ex-skier who's been snowboarding for four years. "But after the first few weeks, you're doing tricks. You're at the point it would take a couple of years to get to on skis."

Since it's a big part of snowboarding, it helps if beginners first learn how to fall. One useful move is the **controlled fall**. It works like this: When boarders feel they're going too fast, they get as close to the ground as possible, lean over the edge, dig the board into the snow, and gently fall. They try not to use their hands to break a fall. If they fall forward, they use their forearms. If they fall backwards, they curl their spine and roll down on their rear end, keeping their head up.

Almost all ski resorts today teach snowboarding lessons in programs called "boarding schools." Many have equipment specifically designed for beginning students.

Along with falling, it helps to know how to stop—and it can look pretty cool, too. To stop, boarders shift their weight slightly onto their heels, digging in the **backside** edge. Then, they shift their weight toward their front foot. As they kick the back end of the board around, they're traveling across the slope or even uphill. They dig in the backside edge again and come to a stop.

The **sideslip**, another basic move, is like stepping or scraping down a slope. Snowboarders stand crosswise to the slope, weight balanced evenly, and dig in on the backside or **toeside** edge, whichever is uphill. They rock slightly downhill until the board begins

Downhill snowboarders have hit speeds of 70 miles (112 km) per hour or faster. Such speeds can be very dangerous and should only be attempted by experienced snowboarders wearing the appropriate equipment.

controlled fall *a move in which a snowboarder plans to hit the snow slowly*

backside *the edge of the board under the snowboarder's heels*

sideslip *a way of scraping, stepping, and sliding sideways down a slope*

toeside *the edge of the snowboard under the snowboarder's toes*

LEARNING EVEN THE SPORT'S MOST FUNDAMENTAL MOVES CAN BE THRILLING, DESPITE THE INEVITABLE FALLS.

traverse *a path sideways across a slope*

switch *backwards, or the opposite of the previous direction*

ollies *jumps*

air grabs *jumps in which the snowboarder grabs the board while in mid-air*

to slide, then rock back onto the uphill edge to slow or stop.

Crossing a hill is called a **traverse**. Standing sideways to the slope, the riders balance evenly over the uphill edge, then shift their weight slightly over their front foot. They then turn their shoulders slightly downhill. Once across the hill and stopped, they can traverse **switch**. This time they lead with the foot that was previously in back.

Once snowboarders master these basic moves, they're ready for the snowboarding breakthrough: turns. Snowboarding is famous for **ollies** and **air grabs** and other breathtaking freestyle moves, but turns are where snowboarders get their first thrills. To turn, snowboarders shift their weight from front to back and from backside to toeside. They should also turn their heads in the direction they want to go and swing their shoulders and hips for balance.

Let the Games Begin

The first unofficial world snowboard championships took place in Soda Springs, California, in 1983. Two years later, Jake Burton moved the National Snow Surfing Championships to Stratton Mountain, Vermont, where they are still held today.

In 1995, the X Games, a made-for-television "extreme" sports extravaganza, brought competitive and highly acrobatic snowboarding to millions of viewers. It also brought big prize money and recognition to snowboarders such as Tina Dixon, Peter Line, and Shaun Palmer. The Federation Internationale de Ski (FIS) governs world snowboard competitions, including those in the Olympics. It has established seven official events.

The first Olympic snowboard gold medalists were Ross Rebagliati (Canada, men's slalom), Karine Ruby (France, women's slalom), Gian Simmen (Switzerland, men's halfpipe), and Nicola Thost (Germany, women's halfpipe).

The super G is a one-run downhill event involving high-speed turns. Giant slalom is a steep downhill run with turns through gates. It involves runs on two different downhill courses. Racers' times on both

courses are added to determine the winner. In parallel slalom, two boarders race on identical courses next to each other, then switch. Parallel giant slalom is a combination of giant slalom and parallel slalom.

In the halfpipe, snowboarders perform a series of jumps, twists, and other maneuvers in (and above) a halfpipe. They are judged on difficulty and style. An outgrowth of skateboarding, halfpipe is considered the heart and soul of snowboarding.

Shaun Palmer did the first 540-degree (one and a half revolutions) turn in a halfpipe competition. Professional snowboarder Terje Haakonsen of Norway has done a 1080 (three revolutions).

Big air is a similar freestyle event that involves ramps. Snowboard cross is also called boardercross or boarder X. In this event, riders race in groups of four to six on a course that

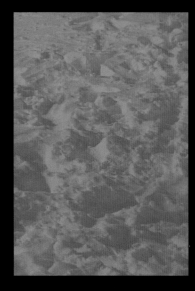

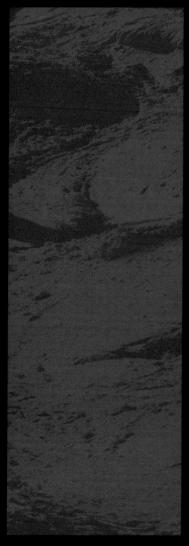

includes turns, **moguls**, and other

terrain hazards. It has the added

attraction of body contact and

collisions.

*Ross Rebagliati's 1998
Olympic gold medal was
taken away after he failed a
drug test. He got it back,
however, after officials
couldn't agree on a penalty.
He argued that he probably
inhaled marijuana smoke
accidentally at a party.*

Because snowboarders are cre-

ative and adventuresome types, new events are being intro-

duced all the time. One such event is slopestyle. Using the

slopestyle, boarders maneuver through a course with obsta-

cles much like those found in a skateboard park. Many

slopestyle courses feature railslides. Railslides are metal or

wooden bars, or even downed trees, that snowboarders slide

down. The move is much like that used by skateboarders

who "grind" down handrails. In one type of extreme compe-

tition, boarders race down backcountry slopes, sometimes

on courses they chart from helicopters.

Redefining the Sport

■——————■

Jake Burton Carpenter, one of snowboarding's pioneers, worked hard to keep snowboarding from becoming merely a passing fad. He took the Snurfer, which was considered a toy, and developed it into a piece of high-performance sports equipment. At the same time, he helped organize—and won—some of the earliest snowboard competitions. He also pushed ski resorts to open their hills to snowboarders.

With snowboarding's tremendous rise in popularity, some snowboarders are being lured by the entertainment industry. Snowboarding pioneer Tom Sims once worked as a stunt double in Hollywood for a James Bond movie.

His efforts helped get snowboarding recognized as a sport. But beyond competition, snowboarding will always be something people enjoy on their own, without referees, clocks, or scores.

Early on, Burton seemed to have recognized that youthful appeal. "Snowboarding is not a sport your parents or some coach shoved down your throat," he said. "We all understand that it's simply about having fun."